ON LIFE, DEATH AND SOCIETY

POETRY

NILANJANA DAS BARMAN

Dedicated to those on the streets, picketing at the crossroads or begging at the crossroads, some we ignore, some are forced to notice and some we wish to avoid- a mixed bag of humanity dragging an existence between life and death, an amalgam of opportunity which we call society

Contents

Preface *vii*

Acknowledgements *ix*

On Life And Death

1. The Roller Coaster Of Life 3
2. Disappointments And Success 5
3. Dancing In The Rain 7
4. Making A Mess 8
5. Unfair 9
6. Un-life 10
7. Time: A Friend 11
8. Time: A Teacher 13
9. Time: A Killer 14
10. Time: The Doorkeeper 16

On Society

11. Tradition And Culturism 21
12. National Culture 22
13. Racism 24
14. Corruption 27
15. Drugs 29
16. Homeless 31
17. Human Rights 33
18. Peace 35
19. Education 38
20. Equality 40

Contents

About The Author 43

Preface

This collection of twenty poems has been taken from a larger collection of poetry. A similar collection was published earlier as "On Varying Experience" under the pseudonym of Anavah Moses. A still third volume can be found under the same pen name titled "Distillations" under the NLHF publication.

All of these were written as a daily exercise over six months in a series of emails exchanged between two perfect strangers. The eight-thousand-kilometre distance did manage to tear us apart. Kolkata and London are on two continents. What came out of that acquaintance is an exercise in empathy.

These twenty poems explore various situations and circumstances, often in the extremeand bring out the beauty and travesty of life. Written from a perspective of a Bengali writer catering to a British audience, these are topics relevant on a global basis.

Nilanjana Das Barman

Date 16.06.22

Acknowledgements

I must thank those who are on the journey with me right now. I thank my better half who is a constant encouragement in my walk of faith and with whom I hope to share eternity in heaven. I thank my friends and colleagues who have encouraged me in ways they do not even realize. And I thank my family for accepting me as I am. Many teachers came in my journey in faith, and I must acknowledge the contribution of each and everyone. But as I do it all I must thank Jesus for this life, this purpose, and His love.

Lastly, I would also like to thank you, the reader who picked up this book and believed in me!

On Life and Death

1. The Roller Coaster of Life

Waves receding, silence pleading,
Tsunamis threatening to explode
Times that are changing, situations arranging
Adapt, acquaint, explore.

The thrill of peeking, tears and shrieking
Pounding of hearts immature
Breaths abated, hopes that have waited
Expectations dulled and demure

Up and down, in for the ride
Every turn waits a lurking surprise
Falling and fading, rising and grazing
Every moment a fleeting prize

And suddenly the earth, is shaken and stirred
The world turned on its head

Holding on tight, fight or flight
Endurance or a grotesque death

No one knows when, the ride will end
A roller coaster of errors and amends
No one lives, only to endure
A life of assumption and pretend

2. Disappointments and Success

The darkest of skies with the dimmest of stars-
Vying for prominence around the black hole of time:
Life is a canvas where the sun rarely shines.

The sunrise is beautiful to watch:
Colours exploding from a darkened horizon,
Darkness retreating stealthily into its dungeon.

The sunrise is beautiful but much more the sunset-
Darkness conspiring with a zealous vengeance,
Creeping in to take its place on the throne of oblivion.

The Darkness it is where reality reigns,
In greys and blacks and the concealing shades,
Life plays out is silent charades.

Darkness to darkness, opportunity hides,
In the bleak dull glow of a floating planet,
Disappointments vie to as the cause of tragedy.

Life is perhaps one smooth glide-
From hopelessness to despair and back,
Joy helps to fill up the miniscule gaps.

A series of disappointments sprinkled with a rare success,
And the moments that tie it all together in random orbit,
Life continues to circumvent possibilities.

3. Dancing in the Rain

It's a quiet day in the field, every day, and every field-
There is laughter; there is frivolity in the young voices that trilled.
Distant thunder rumbling beyond the hills of frustration-
It is all a game, all a play, everything a juvenile fixation.
Life is not in the moments waiting to be lived beyond time-
Every smile, every sigh, every reason and every rhyme,
Takes you a step closer to the stories waiting a telling;
Everest lay in patience hoping for feet to go scaling.
Do you simply sit for the mountain to come down?
Do you simply stare or in helplessness you frown?
Are kingdoms won in hope, wishes procuring a crown?
Thunder clouds still rumble, making music for the feet,
Titter tatter of raindrops suddenly a magic beat,
Why not embrace possibilities before bowing to defeat?

4. Making a Mess

Life is defined in the simple smile,
But we count the muscles that distort the face.
Life is lived between two distant sighs
But we count the moments running the race

Life is held in a clear crystal stream,
Dancing with the light of possibility-
But life we curse in the spiteful gleam,
That strips us of our gentility.

Life is really a simple passage of time,
Held together by moods and memories,
Life is the horizon, one smooth line,
But we keep ourselves drowned in the seas.

We complicate life in the living of it,
Dissecting the good and the bad,
Never seeing the contrast in the image lit,
Enriched through the happy and sad.

5. Unfair

She blossomed hoping for bright morning rays-
Dark clouds greeted her.
It was one of those days.

She waited,
For the merry birds and bees,
But was plucked carelessly,
Squished,
Leaving a bright red stain on tortured lips.

Life can be so unfair,
Thorns hiding in shadowy foliage-
Clasping tendrils of denial,
Masking frowns of despair,
And sometimes even in,
The brightest of day-
Cruel life is a bit unfair.

6. Un-Life

Death comes to those who desire life-
Some are plucked raw and some when ripe,
And then a failing heart lingers with a vicelike hold,
Death is welcome before the blood grows cold.
Mercy, so gentle, in a silent breath,
A serpentine vice of a moral wreath,
Mercy, kind in intent, not in deed,
Often lays into the soil of guilt a seed.
If life were a divine gift to cherish,
Why does misery and helplessness flourish?
Why does hopelessness despair nourish?
Euthanasia: a pointing finger at your sanity-
A glaring question for an evolving humanity,
Or a quick relief for a crumbling vanity?

7. Time: A Friend

Time is a true friend-
It walks by your side in the darkest of days,
Hours turn to aeons as hand in hand,
You cross the marsh and meadows.
Time turns to no one's side,
But walks in silence beside you.

❧❧❧

There are days when you wish to give up,
Life is so unfair and the day so harsh,
Time stands his ground and never let go,
You know who is on your side,
The moment you wake up,
Expedient time never slows.

❧❧❧

Sometimes you want to betray his trust,
Give up, surrender, or simply let lose,
You try to run from him in a hope,
That time will stand still, waiting for you.
But time waits for no one,
He walks with you.

And then there are when you can't take it,
You walk out in a huff.
Arguments range from anything to anything,
Time stands stoically in his difference.
And you so much want to despair
If you only knew what he knows!

Time picks up your messes,
Discarding the relics of disasters,
Salvaging the remains of antiquity,
To let you have something to build on,
Time doesn't keep score of what you lost,
It only keeps your memories.

8. Time: A Teacher

All of time balanced on the knife edge of the present,
Teetering on the promises of the glowing horizon,
Dreams buoyed down by the sombre history-
Tragedies redeemed by the hope beyond sorrow,
And time runs its course in the midst of it.
From yesterday, today till the ever elusive morrow,
Trying to paint a picture in sand, molten and solid-
The crystal ball of possibility leads on a strange path,
Where hopes are morphed into ambitions and goals,
Where regrets are translated into lessons well learned,
And the present exists as a harbour that gives succour,
To all that is and to all that ever can ever be.

9. Time: A Killer

Time is the ultimate killer,
Not guns and definitely not knives,
It creeps up when you are not looking,
It quietly sits by claiming its prize.
It does not startle its innocent prey.
It observes with the keenest eyes.
And when you forget it's there,
At that very moment it strikes.

Time is the ultimate killer,
Not psychopaths or maniacs,
It need not have any remorse,
It does not ever fumble in its tracks,
It takes away not just empty lives,
It takes away memories and tears.
Time does not stop to gloat.
Opportunities lie everywhere.

Time is the ultimate killer,
And as if lives were not enough to kill,

It kills away hopes and aspirations,
It vanquishes dreams, dialogues stills.
Relationships crumble in its wake,
Homes scatter, countries break.
Time scoffs at the futility of it all.
Time again stoops to mend.

Time is the ultimate killer.
It uses the innocents and the fools,
It chooses wind to fell the mighty oak,
To destroy the hills water is its tool,
Assault and repeat, no time to recover,
Time has a very effective ploy,
The surest of fortress it penetrates,
Every security it turns into a Troy.

Time is the ultimate killer,
Because it doesn't just kill,
It eliminates, eradicates,
It erases, it terminates, it stills.
Once time has run its course,
Memories vaporize,
And smiling at the passing time,
We welcome a new sunrise.

10. Time: The Doorkeeper

Oh time, what depravity beckons you to flow
Without the heart to stop by for either friend or foe?
Another year, a turn around the park,
Your stoic eyes scan the desolation,
Picking up the colour in the once faded lips-
No smiles light up your eyes at the revelation.

A quill to the page, scribbles of love and rage,
Equanimity drips from every drop,
The ink of mortality leaves unwanted stains,
The pages of time are filled in hesitant elegies-
Satires dripping in the transcendence-
A portrait of effervescence evaporating in exasperation.

Oh time, what story have you spun in your secret pages?
Immortalized in glory or cemented in shame,
Rites of passage of ignominy-
Yielding to silent hopes of resurrection,
Write a new story from where you have ended-
The climax taking form beyond the tragedy of inevitability.

Another chapter closes with the knell of finality,
Another round of applauses for the master manipulator,
New tragedies forged in blood, fades in tears-
New promises threaded in the gold and silver of opportunity,
Another year leaves the stage of possibility,
Another phoenix rising through ashes.

On Society

11. Tradition and Culturism

Towards a setting sun abreast along,
A torch ablaze amid a path forlorn,
A Hope abated through disowned beliefs,
Ambition strangled amidst silent grief.
A burden ancient, relic of lost lives,
A Dying man's tales, fables of old wives,
A frown, a stare, all whispering to judge,
Ashamed in name amazed along a trudge
Can't they perceive the hollowed walls of time?
Can't ever they tell: future lost in grime?
When is a living to the world a crime?
The yoke all ancient and the axe of change
And time does flow in patterns that are strange
And Destiny sees life all to arrange.

12. National Culture

Bound by expectations,
On a tight leash of norms,
Consumerism raising a storm-
A wave of the current fashions,
Blowing away individuality,
Leaving behind a mindless herd,
Swarming behind the trodden trails,
Hoping for a fertile ground,
That forever eludes everyone.

It is both a hard life and easy-
It is easy to survive yet suffocate,
It is hard to simply substantiate,
An invisible yardstick measuring
Every movement, horizontal, vertical,
The life bound in continuous statistics,
A floating average of achievements,
A cumulative of all failures,
Tallied against every outcome.

Ambition is not justified,
Neither is complacency,
A stereotype running through
The veins of the human constitution.
A pregnant pause judging
Every possible conclusion-
Criticising every outcome,
With the weight of the original sin,
Plunging mankind into darkness.

It is beyond culture, nationality,
Yet always bound within patriotism,
A strong feeling strangled in-
Manmade borders of offensiveness,
A pressure that runs deep,
Exaggerating national divides,
Often exsanguinating-
To the point of disintegration,
The knell of tolerance.

13. Racism

Unknown faces in an unknown room
The unknown makes us flinch
The unknown gives a hitch to our voice
Not quite a scream but almost.
Some call it as xenophobia
Which then turns to racism.

When you notice the differences
Before the similarity,
When you draw lines
Before you can cross them,
When you judge with
Preconceived notions,
That is the racism
That turns things ugly.

Maybe it is not the colour of the skin,
Maybe it is.
Maybe it is more.
But it has to start somewhere.

You take one look
And classify as other:
Black, brown, yellow, ginger.
A colour is a colour no more.
Maybe it is a matter of opinion,
Maybe it all starts with fear.

❧❧❧

When do the differences turn to prejudice?
When do the differences turn to superiority?
Beliefs, one versus the other,
Trying against a social context,
Fighting a losing battle.
The superior remains superior
In whose eye you ask.
It doesn't matter what you think,
It matters who holds the power.

❧❧❧

Is it just the colour of the skin?
Just the ridge of the nose,
Just the width of your eyes
Widening in disbelief,
At the violence,
The horror,
The discrimination?
Man versus man

Red blood creating a stream
Of misconstrued humanity.

14. Corruption

Hospital beds line up with the sick and the diseased,
Collapsed bodies rejecting the venomous sustenance in fake promises,
Children in schools fed on the rotting festering refuse of storehouses,
Because it needs to be discarded discretely and profitably.
Ingested in the innocence of the youth and the hunger of poverty,
Restaurants stocked up with the rotten and the rotting,
Food is food, disease is just an inconvenience-
Is poison a mercy or a mischief?
Food, the treasure of a thief.

The haggard form of the withered postmaster,
Trudging the stairs of the pension office in desperation,
Painting a sorry picture of those government officials,
Discarded with time, rendered powerless of resource.
These bent shoulders are the same that with pride,
In the face of temptation and opposition refused bribes,
Yet under the table, in darkened corners, in greasy hands,
Favours are interchanged with sweat and blood,
Because duty often takes a backstage to opportunity,

Greed often rules the tussle with morality.

❧❧❧

The orphaned parents sit at the corner of the road-
Picketing outside a police station seeking nameless justice,
Buildings with illegal authorization serve and early grave-
For families that trusted the system and its tenacity,
The chain of command leads deep into the underbelly,
Of politics, power and the unnamed forces that rule,
Eyes dry up in the wait for justice that delays-
Or hopes dry up in the face of threats and persecution,
The people's power is led into a maze-
Where the lamb thus slaughtered silently gaze.

❧❧❧

The executive, legislation and judiciary,
All tied up in the string that control their pockets,
Erasing the conscience that founded society,
Disintegrating the semblance of frail humanity.
When did it get to this deplorable state?
Was it what the forefathers foresaw?
Is this the cry for the independence they demanded?
One form of materialism yielding to another form
Corruption runs through the veins of those with power
Moth eaten foundations below ideals that tower.

15. Drugs

A delirium of induced psychosis
Beckons the senses to seek shelter
In the impossibilities of wayward fancies
Bereft of the consequence of reality.

Lure me into an open field
Where the senses are made to taste
The nectar of the morning hue
In self destructive affinity.

Hedonism sculpts an elaborate labyrinth,
Drawing in the future with all its promises.
Walls painted with the blood of violence,
Shadows tainted with early graves,
Needles of despondencies,
Piercing the veins of helplessness,
Calling out to irrationality
In a voice that calamity craves.

Lurking in corners least suspecting,
Poison peddled on innocent lips,
Mammon enthroned in murky gloom
A sepulchre of opportunities.
Grim cries ensue from a heart,
Loved ones, lovers ripped apart,
Christened with tears and ashes-
The bane of disillusioned humanity.

16. Homeless

Home is where the heart is-
Sometimes made to wander,
Sometimes made to wonder,
Exposed to the elements of time
How to survive.

Home is where the eyes seek peace-
The soul seeks rest,
After every gruelling test,
Sheltered from all dust and grime
A chance to thrive.

But when the home isn't a home,
It is a corner on a dingy street,
Where animals squabble for their meat,
Where darkness hides its crime,
Circumstances deprive.

When the stars take turns to roam,

Eyes look up in defeat,
Optimism beats a hasty retreat,
Death knells periodically chime,
But dreams continue to strive.

And it becomes a struggle, a fight,
Living on the corner of the street,
Through rain and snow and sleet,
A dreary and dismal clime,
Hades beyond all shrive.

Home is not just a light,
A basic need for the living,
A shelter for the giving,
Not just from the rime,
But a hope to revive.

17. Human Rights

You looked up to the sun and thought,
There is something wrong about its light.
You looked around dejected forlorn,
There is something wrong about this life.

Human beings prancing about,
From one field to another fallow,
Trying to find a niche, a spot,
A crawling blush, a harrowing sallow-

Eyes wide with desire dances,
A fight tending to the irrationality,
Hands desperate to steal the chances,
Of the need for a stability.

Human paint their own rights,
And deny those they consider the other,
Why bother to yield to compassion,
Why reach out to a suffering brother?

Yet you murder in the need for justice,
Yet you rape in the claim for power,
Yet you punish and then you repent,
A contradiction at every hour.

Laws belong to a blind's society,
Rules belong to a man in chain,
Rights are flaunted in propriety,
Rights are promised but in vain.

A cynic sees the right to freedom,
Bounded within imaginary walls,
A rebel sees the fetters of equality,
Drawn in insecure scrawls.

Yet promises we make in a grand gesture,
Humanity promises itself in peace,
Rights to claim for themselves an honour,
A right to pride and a right to please.

18. Peace

Broken into imaginary fragments,
It is a tussle of ideas and ideals,
Everyone is right except the other person-
Everyone has opinion but not a right to express.

Can we expect peace in the world?
Can we really agree with the other?
By letting our prejudices slide by.
What is war but a race for manmade needs!

Security and sovereignty masks to hide fears:
We fear the unknown and we fear our own;
Peace eludes the restless heart through doubts,
Be stout; The world is ready to fall apart.

Can we expect peace in the world?
Lion and the lamb drinking at the fount
The predator quietly purring as the prey goes stirring
Is it a dream or a distant reality?

Every single breath a burden being borne,
Every drop depriving another in thirst,
We take and expect others to give,
Peace is however in the giving.

Can we expect peace in the world?
When hands proceed to loot what doesn't belong?
Men take with force and innocent boy's surrender,
Women wail and girls tremble in helplessness.

We seek peace within, meditating for hours,
Then we open our eyes and plunge into the bloodshed,
Cutthroat competition and overwhelming rat race.
We seek peace in success but then we move on to the next-

Can we expect peace in the world?
When the concept of peace eludes our own hearts?
We seek peace in the confines of time and space,
Yet eternal peace runs past our fisted bloodied hands.

Perhaps it will take a lesser man to surrender,

Or perhaps that man shall make us rise in victory:
Victory over the primal need for assurance,
To be free from deep seated fear and insecurity.

Can we expect peace in the world?
Perhaps if the world starts trusting-
If the human heart stops lusting-
If peace is more than a fake chanting-

We can expect peace in the world,
When we start being part of the action.
When we choose peace over strong reaction.
Peace takes effort and a strong resolve.

19. Education

Education begins when we start to know-
little by little,
Education begins when you start to question
everything around us.
Education begins
when we start to point our fingers and wonder what it is.
Education begins
when we begin to learn names and faces,
and we learn to right the wrongs and learn the rights.
Education begins at home-
the place where
we find the foremost institution, the first structure that makes us a social being.
Education begins when we first learn obedience
and the privilege that is to disobey.
Education begins when we discriminate love from regulation
and understand grace and mercy and kindness along with the meaning to be human.
Education is almost a simple process but growing up isn't
growing up
Till it requires us to separate
me-

from mine,
and education tells us what me is
and what is my-
heritage,
inheritance,
responsibilities,
all a lie.
Education begins at home
Because it cannot begin
without knowing who I am.
You cannot learn anything without knowing the purpose of knowing
and that begins at home

20. Equality

Death is the great equalizer-
But life knows how to discriminate-
Fortunate from the unfortunate,
Rich and poor, good and evil,
The gentle and the obstinate.

We are not born equal,
Some with potential and some with hope-
Some without the faculty to cope-
Some in a family with love-
Some praying to the Father above.

Life is a racist, a sexist, a chauvinist,
Sometimes life is a capitalist,
Every moment separating-
Boxing into boxes of obscurity-
Compartmentalizing the gifted from the common.

We are not born equal,

Equality is a motivation-
A drive to achieve greatness,
Not base necessities.
We clamour for equality,
But no one wants to be equally poor,
Only equally powerful-
Equally beautiful-

Equality is a patronizing facade,
That paints a world through pity-
Reservations remind you repeatedly,
You are inferior and need help-
Help doesn't come from those equal-
It comes to those who are deemed as less.

We are not born equal,
The blood in out veins count for nothing,
The steady heartbeat is just machinery.
We love equally, hurt equally,
Yet we are not equal.
Because we are not born equally.

About The Author

Nilanjana Das Barman is a Physics teacher by qualification and a poet and author by passion. She lives with her family in their three-storeyed house in Kolkata.

She has published several volumes of poetry, novels, Christian devotionals, and has participated in more than eighty anthologies, some under the pseudonym of Anavah Moses. She also has four published papers in international journals under her maiden name of Nilanjana Bhadra. Under the pen name, her poem has found its place in the BIPOC issue 2021 of the Wingless Dreamer.

Her poems centre around her Christian values and liberalist philosophies. When she is not writing poetry or explaining Newton's law's of Motion you will probably see her with a brush in hand and covered with acrylic paint. You can check out her website at www.nilanjanadb.wordpress.com.

List of Published works:

Published under Anavah Moses

Poetry

1. Wandering Words
2. Sensual Poetry
3. River of Time
4. River of Emotion
5. Escaping Reality
6. Poems by Anavah
7. On Varying Experiences
8. Distillation
9. Father and the Fae

Prose

1. The Disclosure of Daisy
2. Monique's Masquerade
3. Draconian Wars
4. Angel Wings

Devotional

1. Contemplation on the Divine Volume 1 and 2

Published under Nilanjana Das Barman

Poetry

1. The Salvation Chronicles
2. Pain So Utter

9 798887 497655

Printed by Libri Plureos GmbH in Hamburg,
Germany